HOT LIK

Hot Like Fire

POEMS BY
Valerie Bloom

ILLUSTRATED BY
Debbie Lush

BLOOMSBURY
CHILDREN'S
BOOKS

First published in Great Britain in 2002
Bloomsbury Publishing Plc, 38 Soho Square, London, W1D 3HB

Text copyright © Valerie Bloom 2002
Illustrations copyright © Debbie Lush 2002

The moral right of the author has been asserted
A CIP catalogue record of this book is available
from the British Library

ISBN 0 7475 5647 4

Printed in Great Britain by Clays Ltd, St Ives plc

10 9 8 7 6 5 4 3 2

To Peter, Sylvia, Maya and Imogen, with love – VB

To Giles – DL

Contents

Kisko Pop   1

Pirates   2

In an Aeroplane   4

The Sun Is a Jack-in-the-box   5

I Asked the River   6

Trees on Parade   8

A Rabbit and Her Little Ones   9

De Bread Van   10

De Familiar Tings   13

Ten O'Clock Bell   14

Maths Is a Great Problem to Me   16

Medusa's Problem   17

Heather   18

Benched   19

Troilet   22

Associations   23

Mary Had Ptomaine Poisoning   24

No Wonder   25

What's Wrong With Ephraim?   26

Dreamless   28

For Years I Asked Uncle Harry   29

The People Next Door   30

One Thing   32

Shopping   34

My Sister Thinks I'm Hopeless   38

My Mate Fancies You   39

Trick or Treat   40

Today Is So Exciting   42

Late Again   44

Cookoorickoo   46

Let's Go Play Football   47

Some Lines About the Auk   53

Chickens from Space   54

I Had a Pet Frog   56

Nought Cuisine   59

On a Camel to the Moon   60

What Are We?   62

Don' Ride No Coconut Bough Down Dere   63

What Am I?   65

Neighbours   66

Today   68

When Teacher Says It's Time for Play   70

I Am   72

My Best Friend Is an Alien   73

A Skunk Stood on the Highway   74

Rover   75

I'm Not a Kid   76

The Know-it-all   79

Pyramid   80

When Teacher Wasn't Looking   81

Underneath the Dead Plum Tree   82

Glossary   85

Kisko Pop

When de July sun hot like fire,
Den I have jus' one desire,
To run down to de shop an' buy a
Kisko pop.

When de August heatwave frizzle
Up de leaf dem, an' not a drizzle
In de sky, I just feel fe swizzle
A kisko pop.

For kisko pop
Cool dung de body,
I take a kisko fe de heat,
Kisko pop taste better dan nectar,
Icy cold an' sweet.

When de hot sun start to burn me,
An' me belly start fe churn, de
Only thing dat will concern me
Is kisko pop.

Pirates

The night was as dark as an inkwell,
For the moon had gone visiting elsewhere,
But by the scuffling sounds around me,
I knew there was someone there.
By the grunt and the groan and the muffled shout,
I knew there was someone else about.

I knew he had come here to rob me,
Take my silver, my jewels and gold,
In the dark I had the advantage,
It was as if he had a blindfold,
But I was fine, knew the lay of the land,
Each bit as familiar as the back of my hand.

He was caught in the second trap I'd set,
I heard him yelp with the pain,
But he was getting closer,
And I reached for my weapon again,
I was willing to die for what was mine,
Ready to strike if he crossed the line.

So I stood there over my treasure,
On the X which marked the spot,
Then suddenly he was behind me,
My stomach twisted into a knot.
Then Dad came in, turned on the light,
Said, "Time to stop playing. Sleep well. Good night."

In an Aeroplane

The ground recoils beneath us as we speed away
                     from Earth,
There's a roar like a volcano or a hippo giving birth,
Our silver stallion leaps the clouds, thunders
                     towards the blue,
And we gasp in wonder at the sight that opens to
                     our view.

The golden ball is slowly sinking, but before it goes
It sheds its light on blue and white and fashions
                     bright rainbows
From drops of moisture – tears of mist and sweat of
                     hurrying cloud,
Wispy trees stand to attention, ethereal and proud.

The cotton-candy mountains rise like titans
                     on the right,
Below, the azure rivers lap the beaches of the night,
Wide fields of fleecy crops stretch for miles like
                     virgin snow,
And softly shifting fingers point the way that
                     we should go.

The Sun Is a Jack-in-the-box

The sun is a jack-in-the-box,
Springing over the rim of the horizon,
To startle the cockerel on the farm.

The cockerel is a town crier,
Loudly announcing night's passing
To the world.

The world is a sleeping baby
Who gently snores,
As she's rocked in the arms of the dawn.

The dawn is a beautiful woman,
Smiling warmly as she turns
To the sun.

The sun is a jack-in-the-box,
Springing over the rim of the horizon,
To startle the cockerel on the farm.

I Asked the River

"Why do you run?" I asked the river,
"So fast I can't compete."
"I run," the river said, "because
I have some streams to meet."

"Where do you go?" I asked the river,
"And what do you do there?"
"I go to the valley," the river said,
"Where I wash the rushes' hair."

"Why do you sing?" I asked the river,
"Such a sweet and happy tune?"
"Because," the river smiled,
"I'm having lunch with the sea at noon."

"Why do you laugh?" I asked the river,
"You'll share the joke I suppose?"
"I woke the mountain," the river grinned,
"By tickling his toes."

Then the river shuddered, groaned and sighed,
The song of the streams and the laughter died,
And it whispered sadly, "I can't, I can't,"
As it limped along like an ancient aunt.

"Now why do you wait?" I asked the river,
"And why is your current so slow?"
"Something holds me back," it said.
Its voice was faint and low.

"And is that why you're getting small?
Is that why you sigh?"
"I sigh," the river said, "because
I know that soon I'll die."

"Why don't you fight for life?" I asked,
"You only foam and seethe."
"My lungs are clogged," the river moaned,
"And I can hardly breathe."

"Perhaps a rest," I told the river,
"Would help to clear your head."
"I cannot rest," the river said,
"There's garbage in my bed."

"What's this garbage," I asked, disturbed,
"Which is clogging up your sand?"
"Poisonous waste and wrappers like this,
Which just fell from your hand."

7

Trees on Parade

The trees are on fire! The trees are on fire!
Call for the fire brigade!
The branches are blazing, the canopies flaming
All along the colonnade.
The trees are on fire, the trees are on fire,
That's the end of the trees, I'm afraid.

Don't worry, they're not burning,
It's just the leaves turning,
In time for their autumn parade.

A Rabbit and Her Little Ones

A rabbit and her little ones, fat balls of fur,
Were playing in the bush behind the house,
So innocent.

So innocent, they were quite unaware
Of the cat that watched and waited,
By the wall.

By the wall, death in feline disguise
Poised ready to strike,
Until I called.

Until I called to Tom they had not known
The danger, then they turned,
And fled.

De Bread Van

In a likkle village whey de soft moss peep
from under mango root, whey de mawga dawg sleep
eena de midday sun, de cock dem cuss one another
ova de house top, an' nobody no bother
fe shut de door 'gainst pryin' yeye
but meck de nosy breeze come in fe spy
under de tablecloth an' frilly bedspread,
dere's a van dat come to deliver bread.

Every Saturday when de sun teck a break,
de van climb de hill wid a rattle an' shake,
a tired cough, splutter an' groan o' de horn,
hardly at lunchtime, neva in de mawn-
ing. But by five widout fail,
wid a dawdlin' twistin' snakin' trail
o' blue-grey smoke, thin like a t'read,
de bread van come fe deliver bread.

De bread dem light, still warm an' yeasty,
dem cos' fifty cents or so, at least de
mangoose bread dem, long an' thin
cos' that. De sweet bread got currants in.
De man have bulla cake too, five cents each,
sugar-brown an' sweet, an' him will reach
to de highest shelf behind him head,
an' sell yuh some when him deliver bread.

Spice bun like dose in de city shop,
sprinkle wid cinnamon an' cherry on top,
water biscuit, crisp an' light,
if yuh lucky den yuh jus' might
get patty, hot wid scotch bonnet pepper,
de flaky pastry wrap up in brown paper,
but perhaps yuh prefer some toto instead,
when de bread van come fe deliver bread.

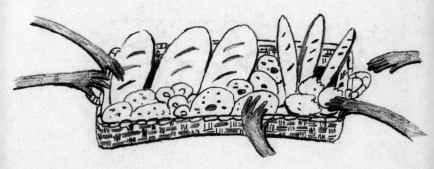

Den open de drawer, teck out de clean linen
fe wrap de bread, bun an' bulla in,
a clean tablecloth or a piece o' cotton.
Likkle baby wid not a scrap on,
ride pon de shoulder or de back
o' brother an' sista, runnin' up de track
to de road, whey dem hear up ahead,
de engine o' de van whey deliver bread.

Whey de village gawn? Which part it go?
All de likkle square house dem eena row,
instead o' mango, sugar cane, callaloo.
And a supermarket dat give "better value"
siddung whey deh use to be a likkle stream.
De speedin' traffic sey was jus' a dream
from somewhey yuh visit when yuh go to bed.
Whey de bread van dat use to deliver bread?

12

De Familiar Tings

We go ova to Spain last summer,
Mum sey she fancy Marbella,
Bwoy, de food did really nice,
Me an' Dad couldn' stop eat de paella.

Mum get hook pon a spicy dish
Mek outa fish that we buy a de seaside,
Me brother jus' order a Big Mac and chips,
Wid ketchup pon the side.

De year before las' we go a Cyprus,
Me an' Mum have tuck eena moussaka,
Harry sey him no eat what him cyan spell,
So him only have chips and pizza.

We go to Paris one Christmas,
Mum put on ten pound pon her hips,
Even Harry haffe agree that him couldn' recall
When him eat a better haddock and chips.

Every year when we come back from abroad,
Mum sey, "De sight-seein' was good."
Me an' Dad always like de beach them best,
Guess what me brother like.   De food!

Ten O'Clock Bell

Ten o'clock bell, ten o'clock bell,
Hurry up and bring break time because I can tell
Miss Wray's getting ready to call on me next,
I don't know the answers, I know she'll be vexed,
She'll slowly turn purple, and then start to yell,
So what are you waiting for, ten o'clock bell?

Is Chile nearer Australia or New Mexico?
When water turns to vapour where does it go?
Does acid turn litmus blue, pink or red?
Was it John or Elijah the ravens gave bread?
Whose book has a character called Little Nell?
Do you know the answers, ten o'clock bell?

She's turning to face us, eyes skimming my row,
She's staring at my face and finally I know,
What it feels like to be hypnotized by a snake,
Perhaps, ten o'clock bell, you'll toll at my wake.
Is that ringing I hear? Have you broken the spell?
Oh no, it's not you, is it, ten o'clock bell?

It's only the ice-cream van out by the gate,
Today is the one day you mustn't be late,
You know I am hopeless at general knowledge,
She's calling my name now, how will I manage?
I feel like a snail that has just lost its shell,
Oh, there you are, thank you,

"Miss, that was the bell."

Maths Is a Great Problem to Me
(Pantoum)

Maths is a great problem to me,
Regardless of how hard I try
My brain cannot access the key,
I can't add, subtract, multiply.

Regardless of how hard I try
My teacher will mark my sums wrong,
I can't add, subtract, multiply.
"Try harder, you're coming along."

My teacher will mark my sums wrong,
There's not a lot else she can do,
"Try harder, you're coming along."
In my heart I know it's not true.

There's not a lot else she can do,
When I multiply eighty by four,
In my heart I know it's not true,
Sixty-two? Surely it should be more?

When I multiply eighty by four,
My brain cannot access the key.
Sixty-two? Surely it should be more?
Maths is a great problem to me.

Medusa's Problem

I have such problems with my hair,
You don't know the heartache it brings me,
I cannot wash or brush or comb,
For when I try, it stings me.

Heather

Heather wipes the young ones' faces,
Tucks them into bed,
Ignores the thoughts of better places
Sneaking through her head.

Whether it be rain in springtime
Or hot summer sun,
There's war to fight with dust and grime
And errands to be run.

Leather split in shoes and sandals
Must be patched. The door
Fresh graffitied by the vandals
Must be cleaned once more.

Heather gently bathes her mother,
Feeds her, combs her hair,
Thoughts of school she tries to smother,
Perhaps she'll go next year.

Benched

Hey, what is the keeper doing?
Why did he come out so far?
He was way off his line; it's lucky for us
They can't shoot and the ball hit the bar.

I'm the one to make sure we get a result,
I wouldn't make that kind of mistake,
Now why is he doubling over like that?
It looks like he's got stomach ache.

This could be my chance, his head's hanging down,
Oooh, he's just tying his lace,
Oh, nice feint, Arnie, now follow it through,
He's lost it! He just hasn't the pace.

I could have banged in that cross from Martin,
I could show them all how to play,
I'd have dribbled the ball straight through their defence,
Found the back of the net right away.

The striker is one of my best mates,
I've nothing personal against Craig,
But I just wish that he'd caught chicken pox,
Or the measles, the flu, or the plague.

I don't want to be mean or anything,
But one hour's already gone,
And if nothing happens to get someone off,
I'll never get a chance to go on.

What on earth is Simon Bell doing?
There was nobody there! What a prat!
I hope Sir noticed, now if that had been me,
I'd never have sliced it like that!

I don't really like being on the wing,
But I'd even go on for Fletcher,
Oh, look, Wayne is down, quick, somebody run
And call for the men with the stretcher.

Oh no, he's not hurt, he's up, worse luck,
Looks like he was only pretending,
I think I'll remind coach that I am still here,
I'll just try a little stretching and bending.

Wow, look at that Michael wallop the ball,
I could do that, honest, I swear
I kick further than Michael any day,
So why am I stuck sitting here?

Oh, great, coach is taking Emmanuel off,
I'm on, I'm over the moon!
Now I'll show them all how to play real football,
I'm on, not a minute too soon.

Don't talk to me, I'm as sick as a parrot,
I was doing good, I had such control,
I knew I had it in me to score,
But who would have thought – an own goal.

Troilet

The city is bustling,
But I love green fields.
I can't stand the hustling
The city is bustling
With thick, loud and jostling
Crowds. It wheels and it deals.
The city is bustling,
But I love green fields.

(for FS)

Associations

Moon, light, house, garden,
Rose, bed, home, warden,
Hostel, student, school, learn,
Exam, pass, work, earn,
Money, notes, book, police,
Court, judge, plea, release,
Breath, hold, ship, sea,
Shore, sand, castle, key,
Hole, mouse, trap, cheese,
Rind, orange, sun, bees,
Sting, nettle, forest, Arden,
Moon, light, house, garden.

Mary Had Ptomaine Poisoning

Mary had ptomaine poisoning,
The doctor felt her head,
Ptold her pto stick her ptongue out,
And sent her off pto bed.

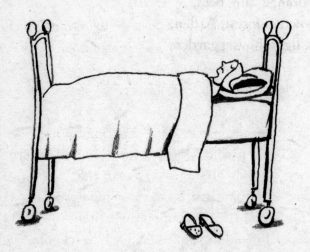

No Wonder

My homework – a story – is due, but not done,
We were told to bring three pens, I've only got one,
I've got a new teacher, the ogress Miss Blake,
It's no wonder a boy like me has stomach ache.

My rucksack's the one that my sister once used,
My haircut's the sort that keeps bullies amused,
My mum went and bought me a purple cagoule,
It's no wonder a boy like me dawdles to school.

My shoes were my brother's, they're noisy, they pinch,
During the summer I've grown over an inch,
But my trousers haven't, nor have my sleeves,
It's no wonder a boy like me underachieves.

The playground is heaving, the shouting is loud,
I've been asked to play football with Ron and his crowd,
And Joe's got a new bike he says I can ride,
Jake's got something special to show me inside,
Jean Brown said she thinks that my haircut is cool,
No wonder I couldn't wait to get back to school.

What's Wrong With Ephraim?

There's a new member in our family,
His name is Ephraim,
He didn't have a mum or dad
So we adopted him.

But he always looks so sad as if
There's someone he's longing to see,
And he walks round like there is a place
Where he'd much rather be.

I took him to the baths with me
Last week for a swim,
I thought a few lengths of the swimming pool
Would be quite good for him.

But he wasn't keen on the water,
I don't think he'd gone swimming before,
He made such a scene, the attendant was mad,
Told me not to bring him there any more.

Ephraim often snaps at me,
He's always in a bad mood,
Is it my company he dislikes?
Is it my home, or my food?

He doesn't seem to eat very much,
And he isn't growing strong,
Now I come to think of it,
Perhaps that's just what's wrong.

Let's see, this morning he had
Fresh cream with his shredded wheat,
A grilled kipper and a slice of toast,
And a piece of cake as a treat.

But he refused to touch it,
And the meat pie that my mum made
For lunch, he didn't like either,
'Cause he left it all, I'm afraid.

I'll have to talk to my mum about him,
For Ephraim is looking so weak,
I wish he could tell me what's wrong,
But of course, a rabbit can't speak.

Dreamless

The snake can't look forward to his dreams coming true,
Can't sing to his darling, "Sweet dreams of you",
Can't dream of a Christmas, white or otherwise,
And when he is sleeping, cannot fantasize,
Can't travel in dreamland to faraway shores,
In his sleep cannot open imagination's closed doors,
No scenes beyond waking unfold in his mind,
And when he is sleeping, the snake you will find
Will not have a nightmare, won't wake with a scream,
For a snake is a reptile, and reptiles can't dream.

For Years I Asked Uncle Harry

For years I asked Uncle Harry
Why he wouldn't, but he'd just say
Maybe I will sometime soon,
I'm not in the mood today.

But I pestered my Uncle Harry
Till eventually he did,
And suddenly there was chaos,
The cat ran away and hid

Inside the rottweiler's kennel,
The fish all jumped out of the pond,
The parrot in its cage screamed, "Let me out!"
And the blackbird in the garden went blond.

A wasp, just about to pierce Uncle,
Gasped, and then died in mid sting,
And the doctor's been treating me for shock
Since I heard my uncle sing.

The People Next Door

There are new people living next door,
They're as quiet as a comatose mouse,
We wouldn't have known there was anyone there,
But a blue light came on in the house.

And sometimes when they think no one's about,
A small head peeks out through the door,
But we never see an adult over there
They all seem not much older than four.

Our dog used to chase rabbits in the garden next door,
But he hasn't gone near since they came,
The ducks in the pond flew away it seems,
And that's a pity, they were getting so tame.

And the rabbits that were always hopping next door
In their dozens, have all disappeared,
In their garden, there isn't a bird or a bee,
Though we've got plenty, isn't that weird?

The vicar went over to welcome them in,
And now he is acting so odd!
If you ask him their names, or what they are like,
He'll just cross himself twice, smile and nod.

The postman who used to deliver their mail
Has gone away, no one knows where,
And that's such a shame because if anyone could
He would tell us what they're like over there.

The social worker went round to find out
Why the children weren't in school,
But we haven't seen her since, so I guess
She's probably visiting her mum in Blackpool.

Then we got a letter, pushed through the door.
Written on paper that just seems to glow,
Inviting us over for supper and games
Tonight at six. Do you think we should go?

One Thing

"You may have one thing," they told him,
"One thing for company."
He glanced around the small room,
It was bare, that he could see.

No table, chair, and though it was night,
No lamp, only the small window
Illumined the room, there was no bed,
He thought about it, then he said,

"I will have one thing here with me."
"No furniture or weapons," they warned,
"No tools or implements of any sort,
Ropes and ladders are banned."

So he didn't ask for a knife or bed,
But something to eat or drink instead,
"And it's hot, something to keep me cool."
"We said you could have one thing, you fool."

He smiled and told them. Though surprised,
They got it from the store,
They gave it to him, shut him in,
Then locked and barred the door.

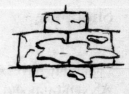

Next day they came to feed him,
But when they unlocked the door,
They found the cell was empty,
Save for some water on the floor.

They looked behind the door and then
They looked behind the door again,
They bit their lips and scratched their heads,
"He couldn't have escaped," they said.

The door and lock were still intact,
No sign of forced entry,
So no one could have let him out
(They had the only key).

They're still baffled by the mystery,
They need your help now, so
Tell me what did he ask for,
And how did he leave? D'you know?

(Answer at the back of the book)

Shopping

One hour, that's all, ah tell me mother,
Ah can't stay out too late,
Ah jus' need to get a fountain pen,
An' a comic fe me mate,
Ah want to watch de match tonight,
So ah coming back by eight.
An' me mother say, "Hol' on, ah coming."

One hour, that's all, ah tell her,
We can't stay more than one hour,
We going get a pen, an' comic.
An' Mum sey, "Ah want some flour.
An' while ah think I might jus' get
A new curtain fe de shower."
An' me brother say, "Hol' on, ah coming."

We only going out for one hour, ah say,
One hour before we come back,
We getting pen, comic, flour, shower curtain.
An' John sey, "I need a rucksack.
But before ah go ah must set this thing
Fe video 'Art Attack'."
An' me sister say, "Hol' on, ah coming."

One hour, ah shout to Rebecca,
Just one hour we gwine spen' in town,
We getting pen, comic, flour, shower curtain, rucksack.
An' Becky sey, "Ah need a new dressing gown.
But ah don't think ah have enough money,
So, Dad, can yuh lend me ten poun'?"
And me father say, "Hol' on, ah coming."

Well, we go to de supermarket,
An' every aisle did have a food cart,
Dem was givin' out sample o' everyt'ing
From pineapple to artichoke heart,
Dad spen' half hour a-sample each sample.
Ah sey, Dad, de game soon start.
Him sey, "Hol' on, ah coming."

Next we go to get me brother rucksack,
An' him sey dat him need new shoes,
Well, John never learn how fe make up him min',
Him couldn't decide which fe choose,
Ah tell him, hurry up, John, before the match start,
We don' have no time fe lose.
Him sey, "Hol' on, ah coming."

Much later we go fe me sister dressing gown,
Dem was doin' a make-up demonstration,
An' when dem ask fe a volunteer
She jus' couldn't resist de temptation,
Ah sey, sis we don't have time fe dis,
By now me a-dead wid frustration.
She sey, "Hol' on, ah coming."

Mum see a nice shower curtain,
Exactly de one dat she need,
But she decide that she haffe find out
If it cheaper in Authur Reed,
Ah try fe tell her not to bother,
But she noh teck no heed,
She just sey, "Hol' on, ah coming."

Bwoy, we jus' headin' fe de car,
When, who yuh think we meet?
Me mother good, good friend Miss Jones,
That's when me admit defeat,
For me mother put down her shoppin' bag dem
Right dere in de middle o' de street,
An' sey, "Hol' on, ah coming."

We tell Mum we would wait in de car,
Ah feel me heart sink to de groun',
Ah know we wouldn't get back home now
'Til long after de match done,
An' ah sey next time a go shoppin'
Ah goin' on me own,
No matter who sey, "Hol' on, ah coming."

My Sister Thinks I'm Hopeless

My sister thinks I'm hopeless,
My sister thinks I'm dim,
My sister does not understand
Why I can't learn to swim.

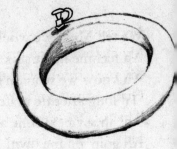

I cannot do the backstroke,
I cannot do the crawl,
I cannot do the butterfly
Or the breaststroke, not at all.

My sister's losing patience,
She's shown me how to move,
To stretch my arms and kick my legs,
She says I must improve

Or she will wash her hands of me,
She says I'm a knucklehead.
But I think it's really very hard
To learn to swim in bed.

My Mate Fancies You

My mate fancies you like crazy,
My mate says you drive him mad,
My mate thinks you are the prettiest
Girl he's met, and I might add
That my mate's met quite a few girls,
He's a charmer, handsome too,
My mate's clever, and he's wealthy,
You're so lucky he likes you.

My mate wants to go out with you,
He wants to know if you are free
This weekend. There's quite a good film on
My mate says – at the Capri.
So will you be my mate's girlfriend?
Go out with him? You might? Yippee!
See you later. Oh, my mate's name?
Well . . . you see . . . actually . . . it's me.

Trick or Treat

Can you give us a sweet, Mistress?
Can you give us a sweet?
We've walked for miles in the freezing breeze,
And a hot toddy and some bread and cheese
Would stop the knocking in our knees,
For we're so cold, so cold.

Can we stop for a while, Mistress?
Can we stop for a while?
We've walked for miles with some aged crones,
And a spicy drink and some buttered scones
Would ease the shaking in our bones,
For we're so cold, so cold.

Can we sit by your fire, Mistress?
Can we sit by your fire?
We've walked for miles with owls and mice,
And a hot drink and toast would suffice
To thaw the blood which has
                    turned to ice,
For we're so cold, so cold.
Why do you start and stare, Mistress?

Why do you start and stare?
Are you amazed by our sightless eyes?
It's just a Halloween disguise,
But we must be off before sunrise,
For we're so cold, so cold.

Today Is So Exciting

Today is so exciting,
I can't contain myself,
The clock is measuring out the hours
On the kitchen shelf.

Mum's cooking mashed potatoes
And sausages for sure,
As she's done each Monday night
Since I was three or four.

My granddad's softly snoring
In front of the TV,
A car just went by on the road,
The excitement's killing me.

A programme about train-spotting
Is showing on the box,
On the radio they're discussing
The price of shares and stocks.

Uncle Albert's telling me
For the sixty-seventh time,
How he collected postage stamps
When he was in his prime.

Outside and just across the road
There's a children's playground
Where an empty swing is swaying,
It's got me quite spellbound.

There's grass growing on our lawn
Which will not be ignored,
A fly's sitting on the table.
What makes you think I'm bored?

Late Again

Why nobody no wake me?
Whey everybody gawn?
Yuh mean to tell me I feget
Fe put the alarm awn?

Now is nine o'clock a'ready
An me gwine haffe run,
Me cyan find me school jumper,
Ah jus' gwine borrow me brother own.

Don' have no time fe breakfas',
Haffe jus' brush me teeth an' scoot,
No time fe pack me lunch box
Ah jus' gwine haffe grab some fruit.

An' hope ah can beg a sandwich
Or a biscuit off me mate,
Me outa here. Oh brilliant!
Ah hope me mum not workin' late

'Cause me lef' de key pon de table!
An' me feget fe comb me hair,
It mus' look like a bird nest,
But me no really care,

As long as me no late again,
For Mrs Morton sey,
She gwine give me a detention
If me late another day.

No sign o' de school bus dem
Outside o' de school gate,
Look like de lollipop lady gawn home,
Bwoy, me mus' be really late.

Hold on. How de place so quiet?
How me no hear no sound
A-come from de classroom dem,
An' no noise from de playground?

Whey de pickney an' de teacher dem?
Whey de dinner lady dey?
Oh no! Why nobody no remind me
Dat is de start o' de holiday?

Cookoorickoo
(Nursery Rhyme)

"Cookoorickoo," de rooster a-shout,
"Cookoorickoo, blow de night light out,
For mawnin' a-come.
An' de moon gawn home,
Coo-koo-rick-coo-koo-rick-oo."

Let's Go Play Football

Let's go play football, said Jez,
Let's go play football with Luke and Les,
We could see if Alan and Jason will come,
We won't ask Harry, 'cause I don't think his mum
Will let him come out, but Mike and Joe's might,
We could have a quick game while there's still
                                    enough light,
Let's go play football over the park,
Let's go play football before it gets dark.
And I said yes.

So we ran over to Les and we got him and Luke,
We went to get Jason and his dog Marmaduke
Chased me up a pear tree (Jez jumped over the fence),
And I skinned my knee and Jez lost sixty pence,
And Luke said it didn't make no sense at all
To ask the boy with that dog to come play football.
And I said yes.

So we went over to Alan's, he came straight away,
But Joe had some homework, so he couldn't play,
Mike came out of his house as we got to his gate,
He was going to the shop, but like a real mate,
He said he'd come play football with us lot instead,
If we'd go with him after to buy his mum's bread.
And I said yes.

We'd just got to the park when we met Harry Arthur,
He said could he play, Jez said, "Don't think
                              you oughter.
Remember the fuss your mum made the other day,
When we asked her if you could come over and play?"
But Harry said it was 'cause she remembered that we
Got him soaked in the pond and then stuck in a tree,
And right now his mum was off seeing his aunt,
"So," he said, "can I play? Oh please don't say I can't."
And I said yes.

We picked our teams then; there was Jez, Luke and me
On one side and then there was Les, Mike and Harry
Against us, and that left Alan in goal,
The posts were Luke's jumper and Harry's cagoule.
So then Jez said to me, "Come on, give us the ball."
And then, "Don't tell me you left it at home
                              in the hall?"

And I said yes.

"Well, you better go get it then," that's what Jez said,
"Honestly! I don't know what you've got in that head!
Well, what are you waiting for? And
                                    don't you be long."
Harry asked if I wanted him to come along,
And I thought I could use the company,
Especially if Marmaduke was still under that tree,
So I said yes.

Well, we passed Jason's House, no sign of that dog,
And we were nearly at my house when Harry
                                    saw the hedgehog,
Just sitting there sniffling, by the side of the road,
And Harry said 'cording to his dad, the countryside code
Said we shouldn't leave hedgehogs where they
                                    might get hurt,
He said he would carry it inside his shirt
To where it was safer. Then he started to whine,
He held out his thumb and said, "Is that a spine?"
And I said yes.

"Oh, it hurts," Harry whimpered. "It hurts quite a bit,
Could we go over to your house let your
                              mum look at it?"
We hurried home then and my mum was real good,
She fixed Harry's hand and then gave us some food,
It was chips and hamburgers and then gingerbread,
"This will make you feel better," that's what Mum said.
And I said yes.

Afterwards Mum suggested as we'd finished our tea,
We could go into the living room and watch some TV,
She thought there was something on we would both like,
A man jumping parked cars on his motorbike,
We dashed from the table, you should have
                              seen Harry's face,
He's crazy 'bout bikes, he crowed, "Hey, this is ace!"
And I said yes.

Much later when we were halfway through a film,
Mum said, "Where's your brother? I haven't seen him
Since half past four and his tea's getting cold."
I stared at Harry and he suddenly looked old,
He said, "Thanks, Mrs Jones," we jumped up
                                    and ran out,
It was getting dark already, there was no one about
'Cept five angry boys. We saw Alan first,
Harry said, "Think they're mad, fact they look fit to burst."
And I said yes.

"What time do you call this?" That's what Jez yelled,
And Harry, the idiot, felt himself compelled
To answer that he called it twenty to eight,
Mike shouted, "You imbeciles, now it's too late."
(We could tell by the way his eyes popped
                              he was hopping!)
"Too late for a game, and too late for my shopping!"
And I said yes.

"Yes?" (This was Jez.) "Is that all you can say?
Yes? When we've lost two whole hours of play?
When we've stood round like idiots waiting for you!"
"Have you any idea what my mum will do,
When I come home without bread?"

(This was from Mike.)
"Have you any idea what my mum is like?"
And I said yes.

"Well, it's done now," said Luke, "might as well

make the most
Of what little light we have left. I say that lamp post
Should be goal. Why don't we keep the same sides."
Then he turned round and started to mark

with long strides
The size of the pitch right there in the street.
I stared hard at Harry, then I stared at my feet.
I felt like bashing my head 'gainst a wall.
Jez turned to me and said, "C'mon, give us the ball."
And I said, crumbs!

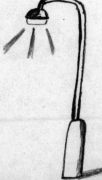

Some Lines About the Auk

As many people know, the auk
Is pitifully shy,
He'll turn bright red and shake with fear
If you should catch his eye,
And that's why no one sees the auk,
He only comes out after dauk.

Chickens from Space

Chickens from space, chickens from space,
Farmer Brown has a coop full of chickens from space.

There's a chicken with feathers all over its toes,
There's one without beak, just a long pointy nose,
There's one which lays only square, purple eggs,
One without wings, and one without legs.

They're chickens from space, chickens from space,
Farmer Brown has a coop full of chickens from space.

First the cows started dancing, the pigs all fell down,
And no one it seems could assist Farmer Brown,
Nobody could prop up his wobbly sheep,
And now he has hens he does not want to keep.

They're chickens from space, chickens from space,
Farmer Brown has a coop full of chickens from space.

How did they get here, Farmer Brown wants to know,
These hens without legs and these cocks that can't crow?
No one wants pork from the pigs in his pens,
And no one wants drumsticks or eggs from these hens.

They're chickens from space, chickens from space,
Farmer Brown has a coop full of chickens from space.

Some men in gas masks came and built up huge pyres,
But when they had put out the smoke from the fires,
These alien chicks like the phoenix were hatched,
Farmer Brown is now seeking a way to dispatch,

Them back into space, back into space,
Farmer Brown prefers chicks that are
                              more commonplace.

I Had a Pet Frog

Once I had a pet frog,
A pet frog green and warty,
He was the talk of the whole town,
The life of every party.

Whenever I took him for a walk,
The girls from near and far
All rushed out to kiss him,
My pet frog was a star.

I put him on my dad's chair,
So he could have a snooze,
And I nearly landed up in court
On a charge of frog abuse.

For my father, coming home from work
(And he's not a little man),
Promptly sat upon my frog,
Left him flat as a frying pan.

I gave him mouth to mouth,
I took him to the vet
Who inflated him with a bicycle pump,
And that revived my pet.

I put him on the radiator
As it was ten below,
But his skin went dry as the harmattan,
And his blood refused to flow.

I took him to the vet,
He soaked my frog in brine,
And after two weeks and three days,
My frog was doing fine.

Alas, my frog grew lonely,
Despite our special bond,
I introduced him to a lady frog,
Who lived in the village pond.

He visited her one Sunday,
A bouquet in his mouth,
But very soon he lost his way,
Turned north instead of south.

South led to the village pond,
North, to a busy road,
My frog was not familiar
With the Highway Code.

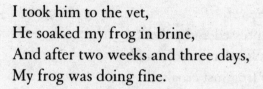

He did not look to left or right,
He did not wait to cross,
A milk float that was trundling by
Squashed froggy as it passed.

I took him to the vet,
Who prodded, pressed and poked,
Then shook his head and sadly said,
I'm afraid your frog just croaked.

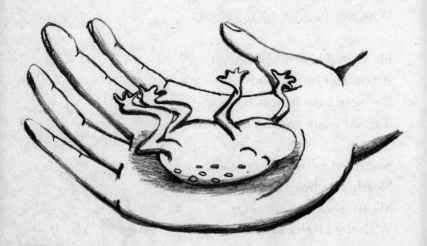

Nought Cuisine

When ah spend de holidays wid me sista,
Ah come back as thin as a rake,
De army could meck ammunition
Wid de things that she fry, boil an' bake.

Mash potato like reinforce plastic,
Her dumplin' is like a golf ball,
Ah try to taste de beef gravy,
But de knife couldn' cut it at all.

Her chicken soup stand to attention
In de middle o' de soup bowl,
It tas'e like she use a real toad
To make her toad-in-de-hole.

Ah not tryin' to say she cyan cook,
But jelly not suppose to go "crunch"!
Ah always glad when de holiday over,
An ah can go back to eatin' school lunch.

On a Camel to the Moon
(Or Anything You Want, Son)

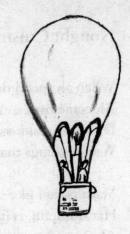

Some people like to fly high
In a small hot air balloon,
And some will get a thrill
From a train ride to Rangoon,
It's fun, I hear, to scuba-dive
Out in the Blue Lagoon,
But I'd like to ride a camel
All the way up to the moon.

I won't need the rocket fuel
So I'll save on the expense,
Inside a spaceship I have heard
The heat can be intense.
I get bad travel sickness
In a bus, a tram or train,
But if I could ride a camel
You would not hear me complain.

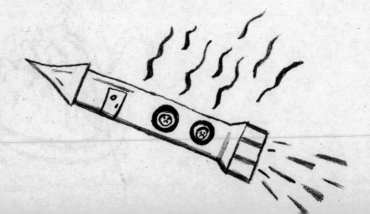

Oh I'd get the greatest pleasure
Snuggled in the camel's humps,
And he doesn't ask for too much,
Just some grain and sugar lumps.
He will skim through rocky craters,
Sail through desert and sand dune,
And is just the friend you want
On a long trip to the moon.

No, Dad, please not a new pet,
No chimp or young baboon,
I don't want to visit Egypt
Where you spent your honeymoon,
I want a birthday present
I will not forget too soon,
So can I have a day-trip
On a camel to the moon.

What Are We?

We're homes for ants and ladybirds,
We're hazel's ponytails,
Sometimes we're smooth, sometimes we're furred,
We're snakes with light green scales.
You'll find us very similar
To a sausage in our form,
Although our name suggests soft fur
We will not keep you warm.
We're avocado caterpillars,
And when we die you'll see
A tasty snack we've left for you,
So tell us, what are we?

(Answer at the back of the book)

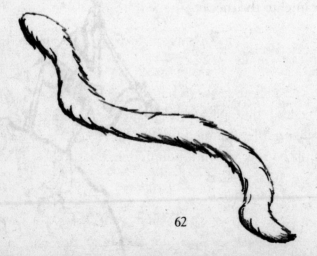

62

Don' Ride No Coconut Bough Down Dere

Papa face serious, him say, "Dere's no way,
Ah want any o' yuh to go out an' play
An' mash up me yam hill dem down dey,
Specially wid unoo coconut bough."

De hill so steep an' long an' slippery,
We could hear dat hill a-call out to we,
We could hear it a-say, "Come slide down me,
Yuh know yuh want to do it now."

De yam vine dem twist roun' de hog plum tree,
Dem turn dem likkle face to we,
Dem say to Lainey, Bonnie an' to me,
 "Memba whey yuh fada say."

De coconut bough dem waitin' dere
Say, "Don' lissen to dem vine, yuh hear,
Yuh puppa really mean nex' year,
Him neva mean today."

We fin' some bough, jus' what we need,
Head big an' solid, perfec' fe speed,
Me in de middle, Bonnie in de lead,
We jump pon we coconut bough dem.

An' den we all begin fe race,
De breeze like razor pon we face,
We feget 'bout goin' slow in case,
We break off Papa yam stem.

De t'ree o' we an' de dog, Puppy,
Fly down de hill pass de pear tree,
Tear through de cocoa an' coffee,
We noh memba de yam no more.

Up de hill an' down agen,
Lean de bough into de ben',
We only see de yam vine dem when
We stop, 'bout half past four.

Dem lyin' lifeless pon de groun'
De hill dem flat, dem all mash down,
None o' we could meck a soun',
We didn' know wha' fe do.

De hill so steep an' long an' slippery,
We could hear dat hill a-call out to we,
We could hear it a-say, "Come slide down me,"
An' we say, "No, thank yuh!"

What Am I?

Although I'm golden as the sun,
No one has ever seen me,
I'm the one you call for when you need
Some peace and privacy.

I'm sometimes asked for in a court,
I lurk around the grave,
But though I'm best of friends with death,
I am not very brave.

An earthquake or a thunderstorm,
Even a shout will shake me,
And please don't say my name out loud,
For if you do, you'll break me.

(Answer at the back of the book)

Neighbours

Let me introduce you
To the people on our street,
They're quite the nicest bunch of folks
You'll ever want to meet.

Dan Singh lives at number one,
He's a ballet teacher,
Next door is A. Manning,
The Pentecostal preacher.

That's Mitch Egan at number three,
He's from the USA,
Number four's the tailor and his wife,
Mr and Mrs Hemmingway.

The one outside of number five
Is chatty Miss D. Bate,
She's lived there twenty years now
With her shaky aunt Vi Brayte.

There's the local bobby, D. Fence,
Who married Miss Dee Skreete,
Homes and secrets are all safe,
With these two on our street.

We used to have another cop here,
One called D.C. Eve,
But he wasn't to be trusted,
So we said he had to leave.

That's shy little Miss D. Muir,
In front of number eight,
Next door is Mr B. Hind,
Bless him, he's always late.

Mr Isher at twelve is a cleaner,
And his first name is Paul.
Me? I live at number nine,
And I'm your friend, Noah Hall.

Today

Today I will eat my cabbage,
Today I will eat my sprouts,
Today I will swallow my cauliflower
And not spit a single bit out.

Today I will not hit my sister,
Today I will not call her names,
Like toad-face, spotty, walrus rump,
I'll let her join in my games.

Today I'll not argue with Mum,
When she tells me to tidy my room,
I'll not take my sword into her rose bed,
And chop off all the blooms.

Today, no matter how much I long
To sit on my brother, Percy,
And pummel him until he cries
(On his knees) to me for mercy.

However much I want this,
I will restrain myself,
Instead I'll listen to him read,
Help Dad put up a shelf.

I'll let Amy play with my gameboy,
I'll return her tape which I hid,
Today I'll try to put right
All of the wrongs I did.

I will not give cause for complaint,
I'll not act like a twit,
For tomorrow's my birthday. I just hope
The presents will be worth it.

When Teacher Says It's Time for Play

When teacher says it's time for play,
And you shuffle out to see the day
Glowering at you through snow-filled eyes,
When scowling clouds handcuff the skies,
And the bully, Wind, with fists of ice
Is waiting with Sleet, his accomplice,
To rob you of each painful breath
With a frosted punch, when even death
Would be preferable to the constant pain
Of frozen toes and ice-capped brain,
When all through break you dare not linger,
For fear of losing nose and finger,
To hungry winter's spiteful bite,
When you get caught in a snowball fight,
Which leaves you shivering, your teeth chattering,
And muffled laughter and crockery clattering,
Direct your eyes to the staffroom, where
Your teacher's sitting in an easy chair,
Lazily sipping piping tea.
(Life is hardly fair, you see.)

70

You bend down to lace up your shoe,
And your knees have turned a purpley blue,
If you wonder 'bout this violation,
Of your right to warmth, it's regulation,
Children, they say, must have fresh air.
There's not much you can do, I fear,
Except imagine you're in a sauna,
And pray that spring's around the corner.

I Am

Where sun dances with the shadows,
Shifting like a hologram,
Where the dark and light join forces,
That is where I am.

When the warm air suddenly shivers,
When you feel there's someone near,
When a soundless footfall echoes,
It's my footstep you can hear.

As a thought, winged like a swallow,
As a sigh that's soft with love,
Like a wish, a hope, a prayer,
That is how I move.

The old man hobbling by on crutches,
The newborn baby in the pram,
The parson, pauper, prince and pageboy,
All of these, I am.

My Best Friend Is an Alien

My best friend is an alien,
Must have come down from the skies,
She tries to fit in, but I know
She's an alien in disguise.

My best friend is an alien,
I say it sorrowfully,
There are vital pieces missing
From her anatomy.

My best friend is an alien,
With tiny toes on her feet,
Her ears and nose are barely there,
My best friend's incomplete.

My best friend is an alien,
A changeling, swapped at birth,
She has two hands instead of three,
I think my best friend is from Earth.

A Skunk Stood on the Highway

A skunk stood on the highway,
Saw a monster tortoise with a shell
As big as a small mountain,
Heard its voice like a loud bombshell.

The skunk stood still on the highway,
Uncorked his odorous scent,
It was the only way, he knew,
To win an argument.

No creature could brave his odour,
Alas, poor skunk, farewell,
No one had thought to tell him,
That juggernauts can't smell.

Rover

Our pet Rover is fearless,
If it's necessary he'll bite,
So we know we are safe from burglars
When we go to bed at night.

Rover likes to chew a bone,
The butcher's his best mate,
He has a beautiful kennel
With his name on a brass plate.

He has dog biscuits with his meals,
As a kind of appetizer,
He thinks he's an Alsation,
And I don't make him any wiser.

For he's a first-rate guard dog,
His bark's such a moral booster,
I haven't the heart to tell him,
He's only a little rooster.

I'm Not a Kid
(Rap)

I'm not a kid, OK
I'm not a kid, I say
I'm not a kid.

Kids have horns,
Kids go ma-ay,
Kids live with goats,
And anyway

Kids don't wear trousers,
Don't wear shirts,
Kids don't eats lemon pies
For dessert.

So I'm not a kid, OK
I'm not a kid, I say
I'm not a kid.

Don't call me a kid
'Cause I don't like it,
Don't call me a kid, I'm a
Child, don't fight it.

Kids have hooves,
Kids chew the cud,
Kids nibble grass,
Kids eat rose buds.

So I'm not a kid, OK
I'm not a kid, I say
I'm not a kid.

Kids are animals
Like a gnu,
A cow, a giraffe,
Or a kangaroo.

I don't have four feet,
Not covered with hair,
Can you see a tail on me
Anywhere?

'Cause, I'm not a kid, OK
I'm not a kid, I say
I'm not a kid.

Oh, quick, Mum,
Look! See, over there,
"Flights to EuroDisney,
Extra low fare."

Can we go, please, Mum?
No need to pay for me,
See, that sign there says,
"Kids Go Free!"

The Know-it-all

I think this child will sleep, she said,
And the little baby slept,
I bet that man will weep, she said,
And sure enough, he wept.
Just watch that woman sweep, she said,
And the woman promptly swept,
That horn is going to beep, she said,
And straight away it bept.

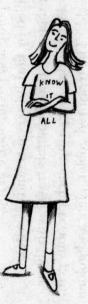

Pyramid

A
Stately
Chamber where
Vast treasures are hid,
Here ancient kings of Egypt
After they had died, were buried.
Grown used to pomp and circumstance in life,
Their every wish fulfilled by faithful servants (and by wife),
They left instructions that their goods and chattels travel with them.
Each jewelled headdress, golden sandal, every ring, each precious gem,
They hoped to use in the afterworld. The treasured goblet, plate and golden cup.
They never dreamt men with picks would one day find their graves and dig them up.

When Teacher Wasn't Looking

Sandy put paint in Chloe's hair,
Sandy daubed paint on Jemma's chair,
Sandy splashed paint everywhere,
When teacher wasn't looking.

Sandy whacked Joe, bruised his knee,
Sandy poured juice over Lee,
Sandy hit Rob, 'cause she could see
That teacher wasn't looking.

Sandy tied knots in Jan's shoelace,
Sandy just pulled a horrid face
At the teacher, Miss Lovelace,
'Cause teacher wasn't looking.

Sandy's been visiting Mr Mort
And he has put her on report,
Sandy was quite wrong when she thought
That teacher wasn't looking.

Underneath the Dead Plum Tree

Underneath the dead plum tree
Where red mushrooms grow,
Over by the silent stream,
There's a secret place I know.

I go there when I'm lonely,
I go there when I'm sad,
I go there when I've had a
Furious row with Mum or Dad,

And when Joan and Amy say
They do not want to play,
When they're mean to me and tell me
That I should go away,

Then nothing makes things better,
No one can understand,
Like the people that I go to meet
There in that different land,

They don't get angry with me,
They never scream and shout
Like parents, and unlike some friends
They don't boss me about,

They said that I should come and live
With them and be their child,
And we'd play forever by the pool
Where the red mushrooms grow wild.

So I've taken my small Bible
Put my necklace on,
The one with the small cross on it,
But when I went, they'd gone.

Glossary

a	at; to
agen	again
ah	I
an'	and
ben'	bend
bulla	small, flat, round spice cake
callaloo	vegetable similar to spinach
cos'	cost (s)
cuss	curse
cyan	can't, cannot
dan	than
dat	that
dawg	dog
de	the
dem	them
den	then
dere	there
dey	they
dis	this
dose	those
dung	down
eena	in
fada	father
fe	to; for
feget	forget; forgot
fin'	find
gawn	gone; has gone

gwine	going; going to
haffe	have to
house top	roof
jus'	just
kisko pop	frozen pop; a plastic pouch
lef'	leave; left
likkle	little
lissen	listen
mangoose bread	long, thin bread resembling a baguette
mash	break
mawga	skinny
mawnin'/ mawning	morning
meck	make; let
memba	remember
mus'	must
neva	never; didn't
noh/nuh	no; not; don't
ova	over
pickney	child; children
pon	on; upon
puppa	father
scotch bonnet pepper	very hot Jamaican pepper
sey	say(s); said
siddung	sit; sit down
sista	sister
teck	take
toto	a kind of coconut cake

t'read	thread
t'ree	three
unoo	you; your (plural)
wha	what
whey	where
wid	with
widout	without
yeye	eye(s)
yuh	you; your; you're (singular)

Answers

Page 32: One Thing – The man asked for a block of ice on which he stood to reach the skylight through which he escaped.

Page 62: What Are We? – Catkins

Page 65: What Am I? – Silence